Saltwater Demands a Psalm

Winner of the 2022 Academy of American Poets First Book Award
Selected by Tyehimba Jess

Sponsored by the Academy of American Poets,
the First Book Award is given annually to the winner of an open competition
among American poets who have not yet published a book of poems.

Saltwater Demands a Psalm
Poems

KWEKU ABIMBOLA

Graywolf Press

This publication is made possible, in part, by the voters of Minnesota through a Minnesota State Arts Board Operating Support grant, thanks to a legislative appropriation from the arts and cultural heritage fund. Significant support has also been provided by the McKnight Foundation, the Lannan Foundation, the Amazon Literary Partnership, and other generous contributions from foundations, corporations, and individuals. To these organizations and individuals we offer our heartfelt thanks.

Published by Graywolf Press
212 Third Avenue North, Suite 485
Minneapolis, Minnesota 55401

www.graywolfpress.org

Published in the United States of America

ISBN 978-1-64445-227-1 (paperback)
ISBN 978-1-64445-228-8 (ebook)

2 4 6 8 9 7 5 3 1
First Graywolf Printing, 2023

Library of Congress Control Number: 2022938774

Cover design: Adam B. Bohannon

Cover photo: Ievgen Skrypko

For my grandfather

Contents

"Water no get enemy"
Fela Kuti

Odenkyem da nsuo mu nso ohome mframa
The crocodile lives in water, but breathes air not water

Saltwater Demands a Psalm

Saltwater Demands a Psalm

Jamestown Beach, Accra, Ghana

The moon's gray whisks morning waves.
Groundswells glide and trade
this silver snakeskin for sunrise.

> And we're up, my crew and I. We've been up.
> We've wagered the winds, traced the tides,
> combed and pored over our nets,
> nursing any tangles or weathered gaps.

Our boats wait ready,
licked in kente hues.
Names like *Happiness*, *Good Luck*,
Nyame Dua, and *Big Catch* are branded
onto their still-banked hulls,
buoyed at the heels of palm trees.

> We've come to shore singing, clapping, humming—
> saltwater demands a psalm.

We owned a measure of horizon
and funked with the tide chasing it
during each morning catch—
before the barges came.

> Before the barges came and scraped our reefs clean.
> We now vie with them for the final fish.

It's a butterfish. We haven't netted
any guitarfish or sandy grouper in months.

> It has to be a butterfish.
> They've been our village's anchor since—

When I was a child learning to fish,
I asked my father if the water below us was dead.
He said, *The water is only as dead as the bodies beneath,*
and alive as the bodies above. He reached down
offering a palmful of saltwater; we both drank.
Swear to keep this balance.

> These aren't the first ships
> coming to starve us. They won't be
> the last. Even our last butterfish knows this.

And he's merciful. He's promised that we won't have
to catch him. He'll come to us grinning and prideful.
And we'll scoop him into a bucket of saltwater, and bring him back
to shore. We'll feed him and groom him, trimming his airy whiskers.
We'll dress him in purple kente like an Ohene. We'll make festivals
in his honor, make love in his honor, and name our children thus.

> And the day he passes, we'll round up the village families,
> and lead them to sea. And with our boats, blockade
> the barges, and bury our last butterfish—no casket, no pyre.
> Just saltwater and a psalm.

Twin crocodiles share

a stomach

but war over food

In this birthright of tooth

and tongue and throat

the mouth

makes sustenance sweet

but the belly grips memory

longer than any tongue can keep

A History of My Day
Bakau, The Gambia

I am without a name the day
I am born.

On the eighth day my spirit
wrests my body's water
in the beat and salt
of the fishing village, Bakau.

On that eighth day, my body
is welcomed outside
with white cloth
and warm water and shea.

On that eighth day, my mother
is the first to read out my names
as my spirit confirms its intention
to sojourn with my body,
not simply to survey.

She speaks my soul name first

     Kweku!
         Kweku!

Then my father choruses
with the gathered kin:

     Kweku!
         Kweku!—

I am born on the fulcrum, Wednesday,
same as Anansi the Spider.

My mother prays that I will carry his wit,
wisdom, and pride, and only enough of his mischief
to bring more laughter than tears.

Closing the ceremony,
she drizzles the soil with palm wine—
the earth sips in toast.

Naming Ceremony

      sɛ yɛka se nsa
      a ka se nsa

      sɛ yɛka se nsuo
      a ka se nsuo

souls commune
in streams of seven

again
for birth:

water's stubborn memory
forever trying.

Kwasiada

for Trayvon Benjamin Akwasi Martin
Kwasiada 1995–Kwasiada 2012

Universe: everything under
the sun, but not over.
Icy red-water, horizon-water
dream-water:
Esi / Akwasi.

I name him Akwasi,
whom you also call Trayvon.

My week's beginning,
my worship—
anointed, yellow, new.

My week begins with flight
because he prays to me
only: *Let me grow old enough
to be my own pilot, to fly my own skies.*

Each night, I paint his
eyelid interiors cerulean and wisp.
He sees himself boarding
an Airbus A350

in crisp First Captain digs:
a deep navy coat and slacks,
overlain with bulbous gold buttons.

Four gold stripes on each shoulder
Four gold stripes on each sleeve.

His silver aviation wings are pinned
squarely; just left of a slim lapel,
above the crease of his breast pocket,
alongside a FMU Lion's pin—
This year will finally be the year.

He nods to the head flight attendant
and gives his copilot a close-tuck dap,
before beginning the aircraft's careen
along the jetway.

The tenor and water of his central-Florida drawl
meld with the plane's PA system, like morning light
mingled with dew: *Ladies and gentlemen,*
this is your captain speaking.

Even in turbulence
he measures the water
in each cloud.

Steer, measure, steer.
Tilting heavy wings through
nesting cloud-water.

Black boy pilot,
keeping black boy skies.

My week bleeds open
without beginning.

A History of My Day
First Stop: Richmond, Virginia, 2015

Pa, this day must have plastered itself
onto your windshield when you first received the call,

crosscutting in and out of memory
with each pass of the wipers.

You must have remembered the Egusi stew
Ma made the day of my naming.

Made just the way you liked it:
coats of palm oil
trickling down a mound of boiled rice.

And how I reached with infant fists,
for the stewy chunks
caught in your beard.

But the voice beckons you
back to this matter of *when*.

The when of blue eyes planting
magic:

melting dark hands
into back-pocket leather wallets—
what strange shape this makes.

One wrong lift,
one off twitch,
click. Click.

Again the badged voice
tethers you:

"Sir are you the father, *his* father?
Come, get him, yes, yes everything's jus' fine,
yes, his heart is still—come.
We're on the interstate, I-288 Southbound,
right before you hit the county line.
Come, I clocked him and caught him, he was zoomin'.
Come, now is the time to prove his birthright, come."

Light-Off

Power Outage, Fajara, the Gambia

Ma eases, eyes closed, toward our cache
of candlesticks, matches, and vials of kerosene.
She places these little lighthouses around the living room
to chart causeways for Ama, Baby Gee, and me.

As she readies our light,
Ma instructs, *When you know a house,*
it's better to walk in the dark with your eyes
closed, so the shadows don't spook you.

Little blue-bottomed flames
whip up a tickle of tangerine ghosts.

And so I'm allowed to skip sleep
to sound these shadows—dancing
in the wetness of candle and kerosene—
with no quiet left to hear the moon.

Diesel generators will soon throttle
and wheeze in those compounds
too blessed to experience light-off.

But for now, on our film screen
of candle fire, shadow, and plaster walls,
Daddy the octopus pins a shaky alligator
only to find the alligator reborn
as a screeching hawk bent on revenge.

Just before the octopus's certain end,
a wise frog overhears the conflict
and rushes to make peace.

I shriek and beg an encore,
but Daddy tucks the octopus,
hawk, and wise frog back
into the pouch of his hands.

I learn: this is how Daddy's
hands hit so heavy, so many
creatures choked inside.

He then slips his finger through
the candle flame. And doesn't blink.
This time, even more applause. *Again, again!*

I learn: this is how Daddy trains
his hands, feeds the creatures.

Daddy ups the ante: closes his eyes,
sticks out his tongue. My giggles stop
as he invites the candle to his taste buds.
Ma has grown tired of this trick.

He sinks his tongue
into the blaze and sips it,
faster, faster, faster. I learn:

this is how Daddy
whets his speech.

I hadn't yet learned
to find the house's dark, like Ma,
and move through it, eyes closed.

Eyes closed and ears perked,
gasping for enough quiet
to hear the moon.

Four-in-Hand

I am ten and you tell me it's time
I learned. I'm beside myself at this

opportunity to mirror you. You
tell me to fetch one of your favorites

from the slouched plastic hanger,
overlain with Father's Day, Christmas,

and birthday neckties. I find the too-nineties
royal-blue-and-yellow one you wear

only on special Sundays.
Then to the vanity.

Standing behind me,
you drape it around my neck.

Four-in-hand, the quickest knot.
Your hands glove mine

as the back of my head nooks
beneath your Adam's apple.

In front of the vanity, my lips crimp and curl,
failing to bottle my smile,

growing at each new instruction.
The leather in your voice ripples across my scalp—

this is the closest
we ever stood.

The last and longest we ever stood
with your hands over mine—

this time, only over.

With your hands guiding mine—
for once, only guiding.

Too often, your hands left seamless memories;
too quietly, I kept them. Kept them

knotted round my collar
in polyester so fine

you'd call it silk.

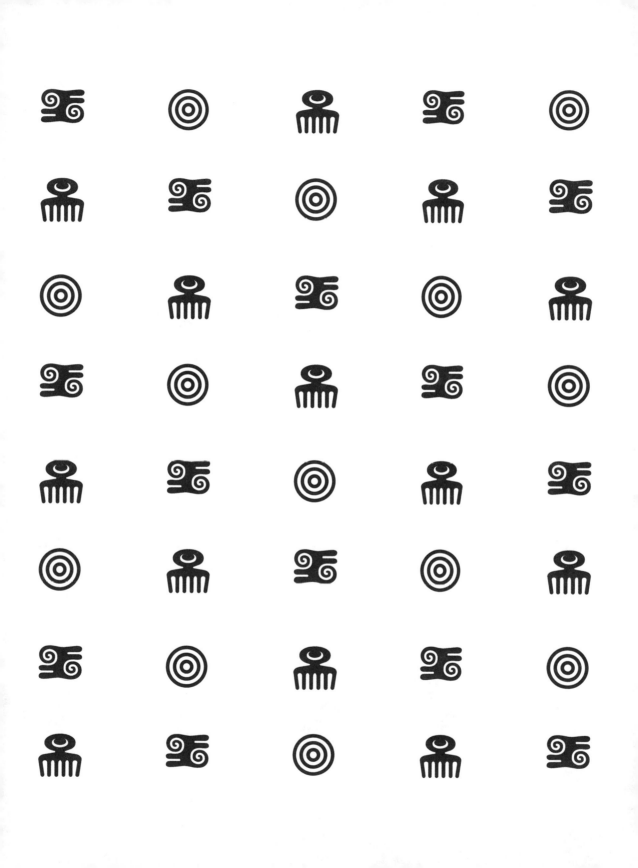

Do you know the day your hair begins?
Your hair is first the remnant of war.
War without, war within.
Next it is the chamber of rice, seeds, and cowrie
          then the courier's canvas
          then it belongs to your grandmother
          then it is seared.
Now it's a dance to feel the root again.
The dance to feel your hair's root is like the Adowa:
the requiem of an arrow-struck deer as its bones sweat
out spirit. In this dance of two you won't know
who's leading whom, who's following whom,
who's possessing whom. The dancers mangle and marvel
one another, loud as lodestars, loud as the locs of Kwatakye.

Burning Box Braids on East & 94th, Tulsa, Oklahoma

It is my job to burn the tips.
To singe them with a ninety-nine-cent
Texaco lighter and dunk each loc
into a bowl of tap water.

The flame licks each braid,
sputtering before Auntie Marie blows out
each little fire, obliging me to uphold my end
in the production line of Yazzie's still-tender,
still-kinky hair.

This act: me sitting cross-legged
on our grainy carpet, sprucing Yazzie's hair;
Yazzie just above me,
on her favorite lime-green stool,
Auntie seated upright on our yard-sale
couch just above Yaz,

whispering little secrets to her
I will never quite know,
will never quite hear—

all the while a mix of nkuto,
coconut, and Blue Magic sugars
the sticky fumes of burning synthetic hair.

Auntie recites Yazzie's favorite
Kweku Anansi story yet again,
revealing the tale's climax
just as she tightens the final braid.

We practice a kind of rebellion in strange lands.
Her hands marry, birth, and bury,
slicked in pedigree—
spinning psalms, spells, and peoples,
plaiting trinity.

In our quiet—
hands, fluid,
and flame still speak.

Memeneda
for Sandra Annette Ama Bland
Memeneda 1987–Edwoada 2015

Sky: everything under
the universe, and over earth,
cloud-water, sound-water:
Ama / Kwame.

Ama played the trombone
        the only wind instrument
                enharmonic to human voice.

        The only wind instrument
                enharmonic
                        to her voice. Ama played the trombone,

                                sang its brass
                                to gold.

She belted up a storm,
        with the Prairie View A&M
                Marching Panthers, doused in purple and gold.

Her trombone kept her water.
        Especially after the two-a-day practices
                before opening day or homecoming,

when the horn section
        honed its high-stepping:
                filing and refiling into pristine rows.

                                Her horn kept
                                her water:

funneling sweat coaxed
        from her lips by the south Texas sun,
                through a globby mouthpiece.

It kept and carried her air,
        viscous from perspiring lungs
                through the silver mouthpiece,
                        through the aching horn.

It kept and carried all this water
      in the horn's spit valve
           until its brass airways gurgled.

Then, she'd punch
      the water key,
           allowing her water

to pulse out, arching,
      long as the arm-slide of her
           Conn-Selmer trombone.

           It is impossible
           to get it all out.

After a decade of use,
      films of water
           glaze her horn's interior.

Such that Ama cannot
      voice a note
           without just a little water
                 speaking too:

               Ama Ama, the first name
               of God.

           Air to water, water
         to melody, melody to air—

    when we say it is water,
    say that it is water.

     ka ni din
      ka ni din:
   say her name
 say her name:

"Willie Bo" McCoy Philando Kwame Castile
Breonna Ama Taylor
Harry Kwame Tyson Moore
Kimani "Kiki" Ama Gray
Ama Ama   Ama Kwame Ama   Kwam Ama
Kwame Kwame   Kwame Ama Kwame Ama   Ama Kwame
Kwame Ama   Kwame Ama   Ama Kwame
Kwame Ama
William Kwame   Kwame Ama   Kwame Ama
Jemel Kwame Roberson   Kwame Ama   Kwame Ama
Mya Ama Shawatza Hall   Kwame Ama
Meagan Ama Hockaday   Kwame Ama
Larry Kwame Eugene Jackson Jr.   Clinton Kwame Allen   Kwame Ama   Ama Ama Ama
Tanisha Ama Anderson   Kwame Ama   Kwame Ama Ama Ama
Tamon Kwame Robinson   Kwame Ama   Kwame Ama   Ama Kwame
Charles Kwame   Kwame Ama   Kwame Ama   Kayla Ama Moore Ama Kwame
Aiyana Ama Mo'Nay Stanley-Jones   Kwame Ama   DeWayne Thomas Jr.
Kwame Ama
Charles Kwame Caldwell   Timothy Kwame

Sandra Annette Ama Bland

Zaouli

First know: a shadow is the body's
echo. When a spirit stills, the dancer
sheds their shadow.

See the shadowless dancers:
see the lyric let from their bodies,
as they channel instead, a trickier linguistic:
thudding tamas, lunnas, dunduns.

See /   / dance, see clavicles,
solei, and iliac crests
whirling under midnight's purple.

The blood-bleak fabric is cut
with white zebra stripes. The dress
cascades from the crown,
down the dancer's body,
and opens like a tulip's beak.

A skirt of red frills stops
this stream of worsted fabric.

And the mask. Oh, our /   / mask,
with ram horns, an antelope's nose,
and coconut skin, makes us jealous
for eyes.

Our /   / mask bobbles
and whines, as we wind our
water-spines.

See us amnesia your eye, your eye
which steals our shadow—
as we efface again, and again,
your memory of—

     time gone
       body gone

Black joy circles.
Black joy ellipses.

See black joy circling
at functions, kickbacks, cookouts.

See the giddy eyes when the circle first
constellates.

Who will become
our first sun?

Someone yeses the beat.
We usher our first sun to the eye of the circle:

Go! Go!
       Aye! Aye!

She stiches gwara
to zanku, *Energy!*

body rolls into legwork, slows
into a jiggy bop, *Zanku! Zanku!*

ignites her shoulders with poplocks,
hits dem folks, freezes, winds a sho-ki-ki shoki

then gbese! Our sun implodes
and scatters this first circle.

Ayeee-A! Sheesh!

     Ajei! Daah one!

Daat one!

Peep Black joy's plasticity:
a new circle swells.

Now a second sun strides
to test the pull of the first.

The two loop and whoop each other,
mirror each other
window each other.

Comot body joor!

     Ayesssh

Go! Go!
     Peppeh Dem!

They remind us that the body is a prism
of rhythm, that the beat entering a black body

cannot leave unchanged. Our songed suns
make sculptures to time. See our animate shrines.

See our lyricful bodies:
time come, body time.

Stank Face

Oh, stank face, your origin
begins with rhythm

like the first ever jam session,
somewhere beneath a tendriled canopy

and near brackish water,
where best we worship—

Someone hits a clean lick on the drums,
accentuating the *umph* of a dancer's thomping,

which then compels the flutist
to conjure a riff and complete the eclipse.

And the nigga on the drums, knowing she's made ,
something cosmic, raises her cheeks, flares her nostrils,
protrudes her lips

the triangle of her features screams
to her fellow players, *Yo you seein' the shit
I just put down?!*

Then, the balafonist, seeing her stank face,
flashes his own: *You thought that was hot?
Peep this.* Then bruh went off.

In the same night, the world witnessed
its first two stank faces.

Oh, stank face, because you're so communicable,
I wonder if you are less expression and more spirit.

Benevolent haint, you're so easily possessed.
Your hosts relinquish their regular speech
in exchange for something prolonged, vowel-laden:

Ayeeee!
    Yoooo!
        Yeerrrrr!

Thank you for allowing driveway
dunkers to feel like Giannis
when he drives with his left,
Eurosteps through the paint,
whirls, and melds his ball-full fist
with the basket.

Thank you for possessing twerkers
when they throw it back and bewitch
the twerk catcher to also yield to the stank.

Thank you for allowing me
to utilize the full girth of my black nose
and gulp the funk of my loves.

Any ode to the stank face is first
an ode to black noses.

Thank you also, stank face, for your restraint
like not possessing those who climax.
Because to stank face after climaxing
is so arrogant as to be rude.

Oh, stank face, thank you especially
for allowing me to savor the stench of my
littlest victories:

I wake up, I unsilk my hair
my twist-out is looking right.
I dress. My Ankara is poppin'
my niggas and loves bless my timeline
with memes and Twitter antics.
I hold myself. A spot of sun
dollops my nose as Spotify Rewind
queues up "Kontrol" by Maleek Berry,
bathing me in summer '16's serenity,
I shoki, I shaku, I stank face.

Gbese

A reprise of bodies forget the ground
together.

>   *Time come*

>   *Body time*

Sweat-taut Ankara, shea-slick fades,
brown limbs finally buoyant

at Zlatan's guttural call:
Gbese Gbese, gbe soul e-eh!

This Yoruba sings sweetest
when chanted together, but it is nothing
without our bodies also lifting:

whirling our knees
like we're stirring a pot
of egusi,

then we soar into solar Gbese
and dare each other—

how long can you remain dancing
when all that's beneath you
is air?

The Function
for Detroit DJs & the Enjoyment Crew

So much depends upon the DJ's siren,
on their trademark *pew-pew-pew-peeeew.*

On their name-dropping, signifying and
scritch-scratching,

even after they hear call after call
to just *play the damn song!*

Still, so much depends—

So much depends
on the DJ warming us up.

On their discerning mix of Y2K throwbacks, new shit,
and the golden oldies that transform us all

into our favorite uncles, yelling recklessly to everyone
and no one, *What you know about this, youngblood?*

We all depend on the DJ's sequencing,
because if they play "Back That Azz Up,"

"WAP," or anything by City Girls back-to-back, those twerking
will grow tired and exit the dance floor to hydrate, thus overwhelming the bar.

We all depend on the DJ's R&B set after the club bangers, as they play Cupid
and cross the stars of lovers and lusters alike.

Even more depends on the DJ's final track, after the club cuts
the lights back on and our eyes dilate and double take, because the DJ will play

"Before I Let Go" by Frankie Beverly and Maze, compelling everyone
in the club to line up in ten-by-ten rows so neat you couldn't tell we've been drinking.

And in these sweat-soaked rows, we groove: two counts to the right, two counts to the left,
kick, kick, hold, hold, kick, kick, shimmy, turn, turn.

Then, they'll bang the live remix from Beychella. And we'll keep our hustling
fresh like it's the first time we've heard the record. After a third encore,

our DJ grabs their mic a final time, but we beat them to their customary closing, and bark in
unison with a motley of drawls that stitch Louisiana to Naija: *How far?*

Brooklyn to Accra: *Chale!* Detroit to the Delta and the other Delta: *What up Doe?*
East Side to Bambara: *Yerrrr!* Gambay to Bahia: *Ainda!*
Brixton to the Chi: *What ya sayin'?* And back again and back again, we chant—

       Y'all ain't got to go home, but ya got to get the hell outta here!

Barbershop Philosophy

A regular walks in
with tales of the weekend
still crisp on his lips,
interrupting talk of sport and size.

The shop
devours it,
pulp and pith.

> *Okay, the youngblood think he got game now?*
> *Man, y'all should have seen me in my day,*
> *I was the baddest cat in the city.*

Baz offers his same retort,
vaunting days of dark-haired glory.

Our raconteur bows to whooping ovation,
then sits.

The whir of jabbering clippers
levels his mane,
sifting closer and closer
to scalp and skin.

He submits, silenced
as this rough, well-practiced touch
thumbs his forehead,
brushes over his cheeks,
cools his throbbing temples.

> *Man, you got the same ol' kinks as your father. How he been doing?*

The barber speaks into the mirror,
where the two play
peekaboo.

Tilting the shop chair back,
the barber guides our storyteller's head to rest
on the knoll of his gut,
applying Kiehl's foam to make supple
the bristle of neck, jaw, and chin.

The straight razor coughs as it's stropped.
The barber invites the blade
to lift each follicle slowly.

Our storyteller braces himself,
a mist of rubbing alcohol
startles his just-shorn skin
followed by cotton dabs

of oil along his hairline
and silken throat.

After a final snick
and spritz,

the barber shakes off the apron,
now frothy with coil-clumps of hair,
gives our storyteller a hand mirror,
and begins to tidy his tools.

The young man angles
the mirror this way and that,
returns it, snaps back.

He steps down
from the shop's plush seat

and pauses to give his barber
a dap accented with back pats—
leaving to play in his pretty.

Durag, or all the places my durag is instead of wrapped round my head

    I.

I've woken up to find my durag
cookin' up bacon and grits:

      C'mon fam jus' admit it, I make it better than yo momma.

If you don't keep my momma's name out ya damn mouth—

      my durag has a quick tongue.

Last April, I found him logged
into TurboTax talkin' 'bout

      You forgot to write off your donations.

Then I was like, *Nigga what?!*

Then bruh said, *With all that space on your oily-ass forehead,*
      no wonder this slipped your mind.

He looked me dead in my face, and we both geeked,

      That was good won't it?!

Shut up and finish my taxes then!

I couldn't even front, he got me my highest refund yet.

    II.

All the things my durag does after
unfurling himself off my scalp each night:

sometimes he tiptoes off my cranium,
shimmies down the comforter,
and hops onto my PS5.

All my homies were shook when my
MyPLAYER on 2K doubled in rating
in just over a week.

I've caught him logged into my Netflix
and sippin' on *my* Barefoot Red.
Thankfully we have the same taste in anime
and rom-coms so it doesn't fuck up my algorithm.
It was hard explaining to my partner how he'd finished
a whole season I'd promised to watch with her.

    III.

My durag is a Gemini.

    IV.

Sometimes I tie my durag regular,
with a modest back knot
like 50 on the cover of *Get Rich or Die Tryin'*.

Whenever I wanna change it up,
I do one of those lil front bows
and tie the tails of my silky prim like a bow tie.

My durag is a plush pink velvet. Which gives me
the perfect balance between street and soft boi.
My durag matches my queer.

V.

I love seeing the supple of other silkies.
My homies regale the city topped
in Venetian red, taupe, and goldenrod,
iridescent as a Crayola 64-pack.

VI.

I saw a video on Twitter of a dude
wearing a FULL BODY DURAG
this nigga is a national treasure
we must protect him at all costs.

VII.

My durag doesn't know he's black.

VIII.

He veils my big-ass forehead, and camouflages
my hairline whenever its more crunchy than crispy.
Each night, after oiling my twist-out with Ma's elixir
of black castor, pimento oil, and shea—
he silks me sure, silks my keep
in this flourish of our making—
a respiration of keen seams and holding.

Rite

For the three months before I left home,
my father allowed me to cut his hair—

a reconciling after so many years of being
unclose. But for those three months,
he wanted me to make him *presentable*.

So I did, every other Saturday afternoon,
standing behind him, as he sat shirtless
on a beige foldaway chair in the master bathroom,
above the sandy whorls of our linoleum floor,
wearing home khakis.

His usual is the Even Steven:
slick dark Caesar, with a shadow
taper close to his temples,
and above his neck.

His hair sprouts in different grains.
Especially the tufts that spool
counter-clockwise from
the avocado-shaped birthmark atop his dome.

But all this close was just
a parting present, before I left
and my hair grew prodigal.

Now, even when I'm home,
my father trims his hair
and fears mine.

Avoiding the touch of the one who cut
his hair before seven sermons. Including Mama Akua's
memorial where he preached the whole sermon
in Twi about our funerary rites,
before giving the altar call in English:

For our people, all it takes to enter
Asamando is a cupful of water
for the journey and tended hair:
a freshly shaved head for men, and new
plaits for women. But saints, I tell you,
to enter heaven you'll need more, you'll need—

Dad, if I die before you, please
reach into whatever earth's below my body,
and feed that moisture to me.

Please empty your hands
of all razors, clippers, and blades
before cupping my head.

Bring instead to my preburial
ample argan and almond oil.

Douse my skull. Take your
hands, comb my hair—
then, plait it.

Surprise me, weave my hair
into something terrible. Into the flourish
you fear. Because if you don't, I'll know.

If I open my eyes and have nothing
to shelter my scapula
from Asamando's wind, I'll know.

I know we'll find ourselves in different
heavens. I've chosen the one that requires
groundwater and my mess of hair.

Though we'll find ourselves
in different heavens,
I'll be bound by that other eternity
dappled in linoleum and afternoon beige:
our three months of summer Saturdays.

You can tell the age
of a comb the same as a human:
check to see how many teeth
it's missing. May your hair charm
the teeth of each comb it meets.
May you collect the broken teeth
of every comb your hair charms.
When you have a handful
of charmed teeth, fashion them into jewelry.
First, make an anklet. With more, make bracelets
and necklaces and crowns. Season your jewelry
with emerald and ivory from the troves of Obuasi.
Keep and grow these gems of your hair's hunger.
Make note of the day your hair takes a new prisoner,
keep this record. You'll need it to recollect time
once you reach the dissolution of days.

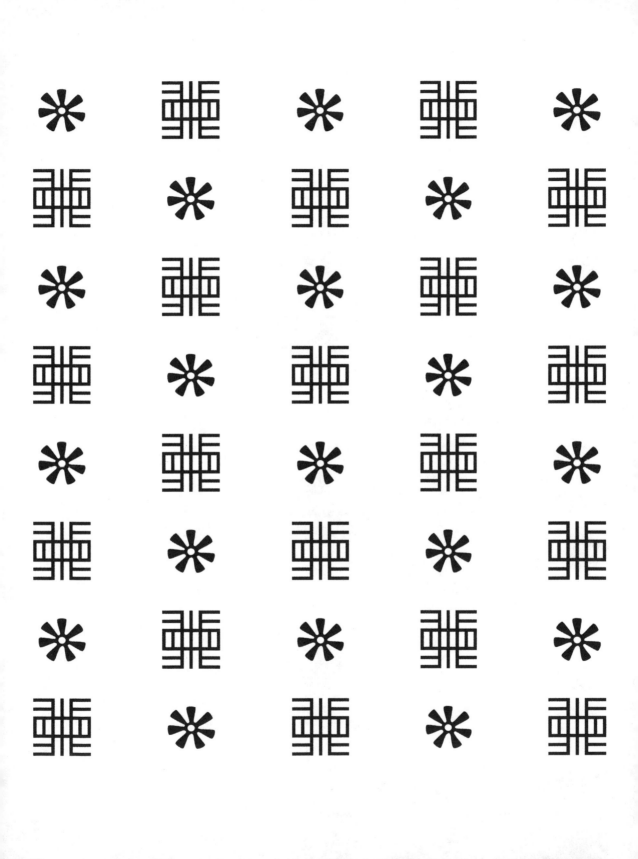

Ananse's web stays us

like how Wednesday

navels each week.

Look into the mirror

of the week.

What gaze returns

when you behold the day

without opposite?

Wukuada
for Freddie Carlos Kweku "Pepper" Gray
Wukuada 1989–Kwasiada 2015

Spider: silk-water, mirror-
water, tricky web-water:
Akua / Kweku.

Raheem tells the story best,
how Freddie got his nickname.
      It was after football practice
      in the Pop Warner peewee league.

Freddie was the same
back then, *small as hell, quick too.*
      Even quicker
      with his tongue.

During the last play of the scrimmage,
Freddie broke a thirty-yard run, wriggled
      through three tackles, and used
      his signature spin-move

to sneak into the endzone
for the score. He couldn't stop
      jawing at all the players he'd juked.
      Especially Chaz, who froze

when Freddie put the spin on him.
Yo, Chaz, your uniform lookin' extra wrinkled today.
      When you get home be sure to ask yo mama
      to put it through the spin-cycle.

      "Pepper."

Cortez tells the story best how Freddie
kept his nickname. The dog days of 2014
      had hit West Baltimore hard.

You could feel the brackish
mist tattooing your skin. Freddie had just
      finished working on his van, nursing
      engine fans and coolant fluids.

He heard the pied loop of Mister Softee
'round the corner, as kids gushed
      from Gilmor porches
        gunning to best their friends in line.

Freddie had had a good week. His van repairs, minimal.
He wades through the line.
      Kids look on incredulously,
      ready to condemn his line cutting.

He pulls a slim wad from his wallet,
looks back to those behind him, and winks.
      He whispers to the kid closest to him: *What's your favorite flavor?*
      Happy with the response of Banana Twist,

he counters, *Aight, I'll grab it for ya, first tell me a joke.*
Then the next kid, and the next, and just like that
      he bought ice cream
      for the whole block:

      "Kweku."

Sean Kweku Elijah Bell Carlos Kweku Carson

Akua Kweku

Kweku Akua Jonathan Kweku Ferrell

Akua Kweku Akua Kweku Akua Kweku Akua

Akua Akua Kweku Akua Kweku Akua

DeAunta Kweku Terrel Farrow

Akua Kweku   Akua Kweku

Alesia Akua Thomas

John Kweku Crawford

Akua Kweku

Sharmel Akua Edwards

Akua Kweku Akua

Akua Kweku

Terrence Kweku LeDell Sterling

Atatiana Akua

Randolph Kweku Evans Darnisha Akua Diana Harris

Alberta Akua Odell Jones   David Kweku McAtee

Daniel Kweku Prude   Markcis Kweku McGlockton

Phillip Kweku Pannell Jr.   Antwon Kweku Rose Jr.

Nicholas Kweku Heyward Jr.

Emantic Kweku Fitzgerald Bradford Jr.

Akua Kweku   Akua Kweku

Akua Koquice Jefferson   Akua Kweku   Akua Kweku

Akua Kweku   Akua Kweku

Victor Kweku White III

Freddie Carlos Kweku "Pepper" Gray

Freetown Rain

before the toubab came
children would decorate
their bedroom walls

with sugar rock from
the rivers of Kono.
during the big rains

silt banks gulp
then burst
with grainy water:

inviting these shine-stones
to creep from their passing
harmattan sleep and soar,

coming to bloom in season,
like the cassava, and the kola,
and the cotton trees.

who then could have known
that these alluvial trinkets
would one day draw blood?

if only the rains had known,
they would have skipped their song
for a season.

if the river sands had known,
they would have hidden
their radiant litter—
if only the children had known.

Efiada
for Tarika Kaye Afua Wilson
Efiada 1981–Efiada 2008

Earth, Wander: everything
under the sky, and over molten
ɔbonsam gyam, blood-water:
Afua / Kofi.

blood doesn't platelet
into purple stanzas. this requires
you. you'll remember her
as an exemplary mother to six children,
because that's all you can find
in english, then you'll forget
to remember. enough. she returns
endless, to Asamando: Asante Eden, the place
english cannot hold. the dead
shouldn't be raised
in purple stanzas, only
to be ——— in purple stanzas ———
finally, you'll fail
to translate,
fail to interpret. and
there's nothing as poetic.
nothing as poetic as:
eno, nko nnya me akyire oo
eno, nko nnya me akyire oo, osiantan
ena awu agya me oo:
aa mene hwan na ewo ha yi.
it's time you failed to translate,
failed to interpret.

Kathryn Afua Johnson

Ottowa Kofi Gurley

Kofi Shantel Afua Davis

Afua Kofi Afua Kofi

Michael Kofi Jerome Stewart

Afua Kofi Afua Kofi

Ezell Kofi Ford

Henry Kofi Dumas

Rita Afua Lloyd

Afua Kofi Afua Kofi

Afua Kofi Afua Kofi

Mulugeta Kofi Seraw

Afua

Andy Kofi Lopez

Corey Kofi Jones

Afua Kofi

Afua Kofi

Afua Kofi

Afua Kofi Afua Kofi

Dante' Kofi Lamar Price

Tyisha Afua Shenee Miller

Barry Kofi Gene Evans

Aaron Kofi Campbell

Manual Kofi Loggins Jr.

Afua Kofi Afua Kofi

Shem Kofi Walker

Afua Kofi Afua Kofi

Afua Kofi Afua Kofi

Afua Kofi Afua Kofi

Afua Kofi Afua Kofi

Afua Kofi Afua Kofi

Afua Kofi Afua Kofi

Afua Kofi Afua Kofi

Afua Kofi Afua Kofi

Afua Kofi Afua Kofi

Deion Kofi Fludd

M Timothy Kofi Stansbury Jr Michelle Afua Cusseaux

Tarika Kaye Afua Wilson

Proverbs: an ode to black advice

Obanyansofoo yebu no be, yennka no asem.
The wise one is spoken to in proverbs, not plain language.

Nsuo a edo wo na eko w'ahina mu:
The river that loves you is what
enters your pot:
romance without finance don't stand
a chance. Love don't love nobody.

//

Obi nkyere abofra Nyame:
God does not have to be pointed
out to a child:
I brought you into this world,
I can take you out.

\\

Agoro beso a, efiri anopa:
If the festival will be entertaining,
it must start early:
you can't drink all day if you don't
start in the morning.

//

Nsateaa nyinaa nnyɛ pɛ:
All fingers are not the same:
mothers raise their daughters and let
their sons grow up.

\\

Wogye di se oburoni pë w'asëm a, hwë kwantenten a watwa aduru ha:
If you think a white man likes you, see
the long journey he has taken to get here: old Satan
couldn't get along without plenty of help.

//

Faako a ësono awu ato, ëhô nhahan nyinaa fore:
Wherever the elephant dies, all the leaves are destroyed:
Death don't see no difference 'tween the big house and the cabin.

\\

Deë oresu su koso ara ne nsôreëm:
He who weeps cannot weep beyond
the cemetery:
Every closed eye ain't
sleep, and every goodbye ain't gone.

Good Air

Today, we gather at the mouth

of the Brooklyn Bridge, to pray the names of the just

dead   *Breonna!*   *Oluwatoyin!*

Names cradled and vaulted to air

but after air   where?

Black women's wisdom cautions

against letting out the good air.

There is no telling the manner of air

waiting to hex you beyond your doorstep.

My mother, an air-tender, kept the air within our home

good. The goodness of this air

is equal parts plantain oil,

lemon pepper, cinnamon, cocoyam, Blue Magic,

African Royale, black soap, black castor oil, black—

Water has perfect memory   but air?

Don't let out the good air!

Because good air is fragile and finite, let in

too much outside and its liable to spoil.

Before I moved out, my mother, the air-keeper,

        hurried to bottle as much of our good air

as I could carry. She spiced the living room,

        culling the mango-warm fragrance of photo

albums and Polaroids; the kola tang of Fela's *Zombie*,

        the lilac of Whitney's *Whitney*.

Then, with all the trimmings of her best air honed and humming,

        she pirouetted, clutching an open mason jar in each hand.

After seven complete twirls, she rushed to seal

        and date each jar. And again, again, again.

Now, whenever I leave home, though I carry my weight in her air-toned jars—

        still my mother pleads,

Don't let out my good air! Meaning *Hurry back in!* Meaning: black children have gone

        missing so swiftly, people turn to blame the air.

Yawoada
for Charleena Chavon Yaa Lyles
Yawoada 1987–Kwasiada 2017

Earth, Power: well-water,
root-water, stead-water:
Yaa / Yaw.

My Yaa, my earth, tasted her name again

    the day she moved her family to Brettler Family Place.

       .

My Yaa, though earth, learned

    the swiftest tools of power in Brettler Family Place:

       .

scissors and kitchen knives. You never

    know who'll come night-knocking to Brettler Family Place.

       .

My Yaa, feared /   / would come

    knocking again, at night, to Brettler Family Place.

       .

My Yaa, never wished to call /   /

    to Brettler Family Place.

       .

My Yaa terraced her home's walls in the foliage of karaoke

    being earth, being power, being in Brettler Family Place.

       .

My Yaa was the first earth baby Zee's feet ever knew, especially when his heels

rested atop her toes, as they play-waltzed in Brettler Family Place.

.

Some days maybe Aretha, other days Lady, or Marvin. They sauntered with steps

so slight you'd have to look real steady, real still, to tell they were moving.

And move they did, circling the living room in Brettler Family Place.

.

She took with her the soil and stead-water—

Yawoada will never come again to Brettler Family Place.

Oscar Yaw Grant

Laquan Yaw McDonald

Yaa Yaw

Yaw Yaa Yaw

Yaa Alton Yaw Sterling Yaa

Jerame Yaw Reid

Harriette Yaa Vyda Simms Moore

Dontre Yaw Hamilton

Kiwane Yaw Carrington

Yaa Yaw

Saheed Yaw Vassell

Alonzo Yaw Ashley

Wendell Yaw James Allen

Nehemiah Yaw Lazar Dillard

Amadou Yaw Diallo

Yaa Yaw

Yaa Yaw Yaw

Yaa Yaw India Yaa Kager

Jordan Yaw Edwards

Patrick Yaw Moses Dorismond

Yaa Yaw

Yaa Yaw

Stephon Yaw Clark

Jonathan Yaw Dwayne Price

McKenzie Yaa Cochran

Tyree Yaw Woodson

Janisha Yaa Fonville

Yaa Yaw Yaa Yaw

Manuel Yaw "Mannie" Elijah Ellis

Gregory Yaw Gunn

Yaa Yaw

Akai Yaw Gurley

Yaa Yaw Yaa Yaw Yaa Yaw

Yaa Yaw Yaa Yaw

Yaa Yaw Yaa Yaw

Ousmane Yaw Zongo Eleanor Yaa Bumpers

Yaa Yaw Yaa Yaw Yaw

Yaa Yaw

Kendra Yaa Sarie James

Yaa Yaw Yaa Yaw

Charleena Chavon Yaa Lyles

Mourning Dance

Please
        Adowa me   Kete me

    Asaadua me   Bosee me   only:

fulfill my embalming

        with the conclave of your talking hips,

your needling shoulders, your tamma-quick knees.

           目

Make my casket unguent with the mist-

        mixed oil of your fontomfromed bodies,

wimpled in a rage of red-and-black proverb cloth.

           目

        Adowa me   Kete me

    Asaadua me   Bosee me   furiously

           目

until my casket hovers

        amid the gusts

of your praise-whipped feet. Adowa me:

目

make mine a floating

      funeral—

bury me to air. Kete me

目

until my funeral wrapping

      unfurls like the entrails

of cirrus clouds.

目

Clouds that fisherwomen and farmers

might need to divine the climate,

to wager the tide. Allow me, at least, this final use.

目

Save my soul the trouble

      of wriggling through bedrock and parent rock,

subsoil and topsoil, before reaching the ladder. Asaadua me

目

beyond the clutch

    of our leathered irokos. Bosee me

目

over the crest of Owuo Atwedee,

    into the clavicle of god.

Bodyglyphics

The shasha of ankles and heels
        a syntax of movement

How many letters
        can the body shape

What is it our movement
        wishes to spell

The cursive of black movement
        forms a language

Of simultaneity and symbol
        kinetic letter-making

Language begins at the hips
        my mother teaches me how to letter my body
how to reopen my hips
        like a tulip's lip at dew-rise

My mother
        is an endless alphabet

Black letters
        spill from her rhumba, kete, ndaga
and the letters of her ndaga
        are as formful
as the letters

Language begins at the hips
            but my waist beads
churn with an accent
            time come
                        body rhyme

My mask is not finished growing
            I must use my hands
to spell my face   to shed my shadow

But tonight   audienceless
            my mother lends me
her mask   we plait our waist beads together

Now here   hear
            sprung calligraphy
 our ink-quick limbs
            sentence the body free

ꝏ ∝ ꝏ

And hear   Sha!
            Our body wades
cresting each beat's philosophy
            Sha!   Our body tongues
and thrums   and blades   and Sha!
            Now dey lyric
Now dey flight

My mother and I are both spiders: arachnid
architects. I have my mother's forehead and hairline.
I was not born with my mother's forehead or hairline.
My mother is the first to tend to my head.
During my first eight days, when my frontal
and parietal bones are still supple, she kneads them.
Dipping cotton cloth into a calabash of warmed water
tempered with slips of eucalyptus.
Just a little press with the forefinger, then a little more gust
with the thumb, if you hear any cranial crackling you've gone
too far. You're only supposed to shape your baby's forehead until
it's bevel balanced, Asante smooth. This is the first lesson
your baby must learn at your hands. Nea onnim no sua a, ohu—
He who does not know can know from learning.

Our names : Our days

Each syllable holds
hours

Each letter: minutes, moments—

Time is a child
a black child

playing tag with their shadow
in a field of juniper—

above this chase,
the sun sips indigo

Along Fajara Beach, The Gambia

The prickly smell of just-caught
tiger fish makes market

Even the fisherman's catamaran
quits in time for supper

Sunset football match
up-kicked sand
freckles the eye
begging a blink

Thatch palm umbrellas
spot the coast
ebbeh red
yassa yellow—

mothers forewarn high tide

Ɛbenada

for Tamir Elijah Kwabena Rice
Ɛbenada 2002–Kwasiada 2014

Water, Ocean: salt-
water, flood,
water-color:
Abena / Kwabena.

Death is not a way
to forget, but to remember.

Time gone,
body time.

Kwabena loved painting
with watercolors, being born
on my day.

He painted my water-
color best:

daubs of azure
tempered with a countermelody

of silver—just enough silver
to mimic my lucence.

He'd add pockets
of butter-yellow: reflective

morsels of sunrise. Then,
with a snow-tipped brush,
he'd render my froth.

Because the art stores
in West Eighties often ran low
on watercolors, or because

the art stores in West Eighties
had long left West Eighties, sometimes

Kwabena would whip up a watercolor
of his own. Mixing four tablespoons of baking soda,
cornstarch, and white vinegar
with half a teaspoon of corn syrup.

Then a few droplets of food coloring
to complete the mix.

Too much corn syrup and it'll turn
thick; less like water,
and too much like blood. He ran

his mother's pantry dry making
and painting my watercolor.

But in the time it takes
me to wrinkle a wave to shore,
he was—

still, the ocean has
perfect memory.

All water has
perfect memory,
even snow.

I birthed his skin
with watercolor,

and welcomed him
in that November snow.

Eric Kwabena Garner

Abena Kwabena

Abena Kwabena Abena

Abena Kwabena Abena

Abena Kwabena Abena

Noel Kwabena Palanco

Sterling Kwabena Lapree Higgins

Dijon Kwabena Durand Kizzee

Charles Kweku "Chop" Roundtree

Abena Kwabena Abena

Abena Kwabena Abena

Kendrec Kwabena McDade Korryn Abena Gaines

William Kwabena Howard Green

Henry Kwabena "Ace" Glover Dante Kwabena "Strawberry" Daniels

Abena Kwabena Abena

Vernon Kwabena Dahmer

Dr. Benjamin Kwabena

Kyam Abena Livingston

Abena Kwabena Abena

Abena Kwabena Abena

Abena Kwabena Abena

Eula Abena Mae Love

Abena Kwabena Abena

Abena Kwabena Ellery Murph Walter Kwabena Lamar Scott

Tamir Elijah Kwabena Rice

A History of My Day
Third Stop: Kylertown, Pennsylvania, 2020

My mother and I are born on the same day
one week apart. She celebrates her birthday
sometimes on mine. Two children of Anansi:
blood-knit arachnids.

I don't remember the day of this stop
only that it is snowing.

The original Akan calendar has eight days.
When Obroni came, he disappeared a day,
forcing six days work, one day rest.
But each week, since Obroni came,
we've carried over our extra day.

He approaches my passenger's side.
In my rearview, a curl of snow
severs his head.

My mother is already Sundayless,
has almost lost her Wednesday, twice.

And Miss Samaria is without
Tuesday. Miss Sybrina's without Sunday.
There's gravity between Sunday and Tuesday
for Miss Lezley and the eternal un-Saturday
for Miss Geneva, and Miss Gloria's week has no middle.
And all the week's without—

      time gone
        body time.

My god, what day is it today?
My god, who day is it yesterday?
My god, who day was it tomorrow?

As he nears, the dusk-blue snow fails to keep him headless.
I don't remember the day I'm stopped,
but when he asks for my name, I chant
the name of that eighth and unforgotten day.

No, no, today is not my day.

Naming Ceremony

The day of a child's naming
is their real birth.

We whisper water
into their week-old ears:

      sɛ yɛka se nsa   *when we say it is gin*
      a ka se nsa.   *say that it is gin.*

      sɛ yɛka se nsuo   *when we say it is water*
      a ka se nsuo.   *say that it is water.*

Water is memory
forever trying

to get back
to where it was.

And ours, parted by saltwater,
parted by flood,
Asamando awaits.

It is time again
for birth.

Ɛdwoada
for Michael Kojo Brown Jr.
Ɛdwoada 1996–Memeneda 2014

Peace: not-so-calm-
water, sometimes water-
in-the-eye-of-the-storm-water:
Adjoa / Kojo.

I'm peace-water,
water-in-the-eye-

of-the-storm-
water.

I name him
Peace also,

Kojo
also.

Kojo
also—

Where are
our names?

Are our names?

Don't call me Ɛdwoada
or Monday-god anymore.

Take my day,
numb my name.

Gods and Spirits
go blue with guilt.

Because
we've never

asked
forgiveness.

I want to swallow
my name:

to practice more than atheism:
deicide.

All in exchange for this
forgiveness.

Swallowing my name
in exchange

for his
forgiveness.

I'll attempt repentance
a final time:

Do you want this
name?

Do you want this name
which is only a prayer,
not even a psalm?

Will you take this name,
Kojo?

Please, *Kojo*—

Please, *Kojo*—

will you take this name?

Walter Kojo Rodney   Kojo Deborah Adjoa Danner

Kojo Adjoa Kojo

Kojo Adjoa Kojo   Joseph Kojo Martin

Kenneth Kojo Chamberlain Sr.

Kojo Adjoa Kojo   Kojo Adjoa Kojo

Kojo Adjoa Kojo   Kojo Adjoa Kojo

Victor Kojo Steen   Kojo Adjoa Kojo

Ronald Kojo Curtis Madison   Kojo Adjoa Kojo

Gabriella Adjoa Nevarez   Kojo Adjoa Kojo

Eugene Washington

Joseph Kojo Mann   Terence Kojo Crutcher   Kojo Adjoa Kojo   Kojo Adjoa Kojo

Natasha Adjoa McKenna   Reginald Kojo Doucet   Kojo Adjoa Kojo

Anthony Kojo Weber   Reynaldo Kojo Cuevas

Jersey Kuzelle Kojo Green   Quintonio Kojo LeGrier   Timothy Kojo Russell

Steven Kojo   Danroy "DJ" Kojo Henry Jr.   Ramarely Kojo Graham

Derek Kojo Williams

Rumain Kojo Brisbon   Johnnie Kojo Kamahi Warren

Michael Kojo Brown Jr.

you must think yourself so big

with your theory

of time   but Wednesday is

no more   Thursday went

missing   Saturday's been bled

We witnessed the day   of Sunday's

naming and the day

of her—

Our weeks ache

for days and days and days

then, what of time?

 time gone

   body time.

The Tree of God is out of season.
The Tree of God has forgotten
its bloom time, due to a dearth of days,
a famine of weeks, the plucking of months—
or the Tree of God is still in season.
The Tree of God has forgotten when to stop
blooming, due to a dearth of days,
a famine of weeks, the plucking of months—
time gone, body time.

Libation

Swallow   spirits with me   many
drink   many drank   many
drunk from this calabash
of palm wine I pour

While pouring I
chant

Kwame   Kwame   come drink

The giver of Saturday
receive drink

As I pour soilward
some of the drink spittles
along the hem of my lucid cloth

Yaa   Yaa   come drink

Thursday's keeper   and   Earth's
here is drink for you too   today
today   is your lustral day
drink-drink

I keep pouring

When I call one of you I have called
all   you departed spirits of the seven
receive this and visit:
water by birthright
water by blood

Welcome airful welcome unskinned
welcome saltskinned welcome bulletskinned
welcome reeking welcome pine-black ghouls

Listen
I come seeking Days

I refuse to stop
pouring   because
I refuse to stop
pouring

Days sprout from haint-
tilled soil   the Days we cannot yet
see require the most mercy

The purple earth   around me
bears weeks:

the incessant rain
of my libation:

the floodplain
of my

Drink! Drink! Drink!

First it is only a hiss
that rises

Then the deluge
of Days
coming back into time

Yes Akosua yes Akwasi
yes Ama and Kwame
yes Kofi and Afua
yes Yaa   Yaw
Akua   Kweku
Kwabena and Abena
Adjoa and Kojo
You well-named

You will only die
when days die

The risen sing
back to the teeming soil   coaxing
more to our realm   uncocooned

Drink too   drink—
today be today   today:
your lustral day

Saltwater   does   not
irrigate   saltwater
cannot grow—

But look!   Look
what flowers
vein-drunk

Awash
in Asante Eden

Adinkra

Our stories tear
too easily through
papyrus.

To document
the deeds of the Ohenes
would deplete
the world of bark,
the forest of parchment leaves.

So, we learn to speak
in symbol, to whisper in drum,
to dialogue with bodies
like the chameleon.

Bring sinew, bring
bone, bring skin,
let us make more
than language.

I speak for skin.
I am the rivulet,
nurturing webs of rivers
from the lips of mountains.

I knew you before
you could inhabit water
before you could count rains.

I am Nyame Dua
for when you see trees bearing men
instead of baobab buds.

I am Duafe for the night of your wedding,
and for when your hair is first broken,
and for when you fight to feel
its gamey root again,
like Kwatakye Atiko.

I am the egg
nestled on your feathery back:

turn back
fear no flames,
fear no salt,

I am Sankofa
     keep turning back—

     I am.

Notes

 "Funtumfunefu Denkyemfunefu": Siamese crocodiles. This Adinkra symbol signifies the necessity of intertribal and intercultural unity. Adinkra are proverb-laden symbols from the Akan and Gyaman peoples of Ghana and Côte d'Ivoire. For further reading on Adinkra symbols, consult W. Bruce Willis's *The Adinkra Dictionary*.

"A History of My Day, *Bakau, The Gambia*" features language and rituals from Akan naming ceremonies. Per Akan custom, kradin, or soul names, are given in accordance with a child's day of birth. These given, not chosen, names influence a child's character and fate. Each kradin is under the protection of a tutelary god.

"Naming Ceremony (sɛ yɛka se nsa)": *sɛ yɛka se nsa / a ka se nsa* (when we say it is gin / say it is gin), *sɛ yɛka se nsuo / a ka se nsuo* (when we say it is water / say it is water).

"Kwasiada": Trayvon Martin dreamt of becoming a pilot. On May 13, 2017, Martin was posthumously awarded a bachelor's degree in aeronautical science by the historically Black Florida Memorial University (FMU). His parents, Tracy Martin and Sybrina Fulton, accepted the degree in his honor. FMU is Fulton's alma mater. In the continued fight against anti-Black violence, the website Blackpast.org is a great starting point in learning more about the lives and legacies of those no longer with us as a result of racist hate and police brutality.

 "Kwatakye Atiko": This Adinkra embodies the mangled and marvelous hairstyle of famed Asante war captain Kwatakye, who wore his valor in his hair.

"Memeneda": Sandra Bland began playing the trombone as a child and eventually earned a marching-band scholarship to the historically Black Prairie View A&M University.

"Zaouli" is a traditional dance of Côte d'Ivoire's Guro people—a dance with a river of origins. Despite competing origins, this remains constant: it is a dance in honor of feminine beauty, performed by masked men.

"Adinkrahene": The chief of the Adinkra. The cornerstone of the Adinkra pantheon: charisma, leadership, greatness.

"Gbese" is a Yoruba command to lift the legs or body. It is also an Afrobeats dance move made popular by Burna Boy and Zlatan's "Killin Dem." A good gbese can scatter any dance circle.

"Rite": Old Akan custom dictates that water should be offered to the dying before the moment of death, in preparation for their journey into the afterlife. Before burial, the hair of the deceased is styled a final time. For further reading on funerary rites of Ghana's Akan peoples consider *Funerals Among the Akan People: Some Perspectives on Asante* by Samuel Adu-Gyamfi, Emmanuel Antwi Fordjour, Charles O. Marfo, and Isaac Forson Adjei.

 "Duafe": a prized wooden comb, embodying love, self-care, and beauty.

 "Ananse Ntentan": the spider's web. The master trickster and architect Ananse the spider figures prominently in Akan folktales, and their diasporic afterlives. His strengths are wisdom, creativity, complexity.

"Wukuada" is inspired by anecdotes about Freddie Gray I encountered in Devin Allen's *A Beautiful Ghetto*, as well as an intimate profile on Freddie's life published through the *Baltimore Sun*.

"Freetown Rain" is indebted to the stories my grandfather told of his upbringing in Freetown, Sierra Leone, where diamonds were so abundant that they could be found near the surface of river beds after the rains.

The Twi dirge at the end of "Efiada" is taken from J. H. Kwabena Nketia's seminal *Funeral Dirges of the Akan People*. It is traditionally sung at the passing of mothers.

 In "Mourning Dance," Owuo Atwedee: The ladder of death. Symbolizes the eventuality of death, as well as the journey between the living world and the ancestral plane.

"Bodyglyphics" features letters from the Wolof Garay alphabet. The alphabet was created by Assane Faye in 1961 in celebration of Senegal's independence from France.

 "Nea onnim no sua a, ohu": *he who does not know can know from learning.* This Adinkra embodies one's lifelong quest for knowledge. For further reading on this and other Adinkra symbols, please also consult G. F. Kojo Arthur's *Cloth As Metaphor.*

 "Nyame Dua": the tree of God, altar. A symbol of divine protection and presence. It is a sacred tree usually at the entrance of a home or compound where ancestral and purification rituals are performed.

"Aya": fern. Symbolizes nature, endurance, and independence.

"Ɛbenada": During his life, Tamir Rice enjoyed visual art and was enrolled in an after-school arts program.

"A History of My Day, *Third Stop: Kylertown, Pennsylvania, 2020*": Oral histories differ on the number of days in the pre-colonial Akan calendar, some contend six days, others argue for eight. It was only when Obroni came that our days became seven.

In "Naming Ceremony" *Asamando* signifies the Akan concept of afterlife or ancestral plane.

"Libation" contains found language from traditional Akan libation ceremonies where alcohol is poured on the earth, inviting deities and ancestors to partake in the merriment of the living.

 Sankofa: It is not taboo to fetch what is at risk of being left behind. Go back and get it.

Acknowledgments

Special thanks to the readers and editors of the following publications for making space for my poems.

20.35 Africa — "Adinkra"

The Academy of American Poets: "Kwasiada" and "Wukuada"

The Common — "Rite"

Obsidian — "Four-in-Hand," "Light-Off," and "Hem"

The Shade Journal — "Stank Face"

Sunu Journal — "Freetown Rain"

      //

Y'all it takes a village to raise a poetry collection.

I first wish to thank my late grandfather, Wilmot Oguntola John, whose bedtime stories and repository of West African folklore first sparked my interest in literature.

Next, a huge shout out to my first creative writing community, the Area Program in Poetry Writing at the University of Virginia—shout out to the APPW peeps Chi Chi, Ale, and Aliyah for being some of my earliest and most generous readers. Thank you Maliha and Kevin for your love and patience through countless drafts of bad poems.

Thank you to UVA English and African American Studies faculty, especially Paul Guest, Rita Dove, Lisa Russ Spaar, Stephen Cushman, Rob Shapiro, Debra Nystrom, Kwame Otu, Claudrena Harold, Mark Hadley, Maurice Wallace, and Brenda Marie Osbey—who each fed my curiosity in writing.

This manuscript would not be possible without the careful eyes of my University of Michigan MFA cohort, Sara, Chris, Ayo, Nadia, Serena, Julia, Catherine, and Mary. Y'all make my heart so warm, thank you for your grace and willingness to go deep with me.

Thank yous are in order for the poetry faculty at the Helen Zell Writers' Program. Thank you especially Van, Sumita, and Hui-Hui for helping me transform this figment of my poetic imagination into a tangible finished project. Thank you also to my graduate thesis reader Valencia for shepherding this work across the finish line.

Shout out to the Enjoyment Crew! Enjoyment no dey finish sha! Thank you all for dancing, laughing, debating, camping, playing spades, and being outside with me. Monet, Chi Chi, Adaeze, Dom, Laru, Desnor, KT, I consider myself blessed to be able to do life with each of you. Thank you Modestea for your love and for sharing your pickles with me and for crying with me at the end of *Titanic*.

Thank you to Tyehimba Jess whose decision to select my manuscript for the 2022 Academy of American Poets First Book Award changed my life. Special thanks to the Academy of American poets for graciously supporting my work.

Thank you to all the good folks at Graywolf—especially Chantz, Jeff, Marisa, and Katie—for chopping up the publication process into bite-sized pieces.

Thank you, readers, y'all are the real MVPs! I am so blessed that you took to the time to commune with my words.

Thank you finally to all the poets, named and unnamed whose words tress the fabric of my ancestry. The days we cannot yet see require the most mercy.

KWEKU ABIMBOLA earned his MFA in poetry from the University of Michigan's Helen Zell Writers' Program. His work has been published or is forthcoming in the *Shade Journal*, *20.35 Africa*, the *Common*, and elsewhere. He lives in Detroit, Michigan.

The text of *Saltwater Demands a Psalm* is set in Adobe Garamond Pro.
Book design by Rachel Holscher.
Composition by Bookmobile Design and Digital Publisher Services, Minneapolis, Minnesota.
Manufactured by Versa Press on acid-free, 30 percent postconsumer wastepaper.